Let's Explore China

China

by Walt K. Moon

BUMBA BOOKS™

LERNER PUBLICATIONS ◆ MINNEAPOLIS

Note to Educators:

Throughout this book, you'll find critical thinking questions. These can be used to engage young readers in thinking critically about the topic and in using the text and photos to do so.

Lerner Publications Company
A division of Lerner Publishing Group, Inc.
241 First Avenue North
Minneapolis, MN 55401 USA

For reading levels and more information, look up this title at www.lernerbooks.com.

Library of Congress Cataloging-in-Publication Data
Names: Moon, Walt K., author.
Title: Let's explore China / by Walt K. Moon.
Description: Minneapolis : Lerner Publications, [2016] | Includes bibliographical references and index. | Audience: Grades K–3.
Identifiers: LCCN 2016018689 (print) | LCCN 2016019480 (ebook) | ISBN 9781512430042 (lb : alk. paper) | ISBN 9781512430134 (pb : alk. paper) | ISBN 9781512430141 (eb pdf)
Subjects: LCSH: China—Juvenile literature.
Classification: LCC DS706 .M65 2016 (print) | LCC DS706 (ebook) | DDC 951—dc23

LC record available at https://lccn.loc.gov/2016018689

Manufactured in the United States of America
1 – VP – 12/31/16

Expand learning beyond the printed book. Download free, complementary educational resources for this book from our website, www.lerneresource.com.

Table of Contents

A Visit to China

China is a country in Asia.

China is very big.

It has many people.

China has tall mountains.

It has dry deserts.

It has flat plains.

It touches the ocean.

Pandas live in China.

They are black and white.

Pandas eat plants called bamboo.

Bamboo grows in forests.

China has many forests.

China has big cities.

They are growing fast.

Many people live there.

Why might people move to cities?

Many people visit China.

They see the Great Wall.

It was built hundreds of years ago.

It is made of stone.

Why do you think people built the Great Wall?

Dumplings are a popular

Chinese food.

Dumplings are wrapped in dough.

They are filled with meat

or vegetables.

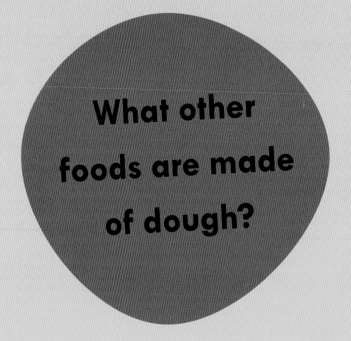

What other foods are made of dough?

Many people in China love sports.

Basketball is popular there.

Many people ride bicycles too.

China is a beautiful country.

There are many things to see.

Would you like to visit China?

Map of China

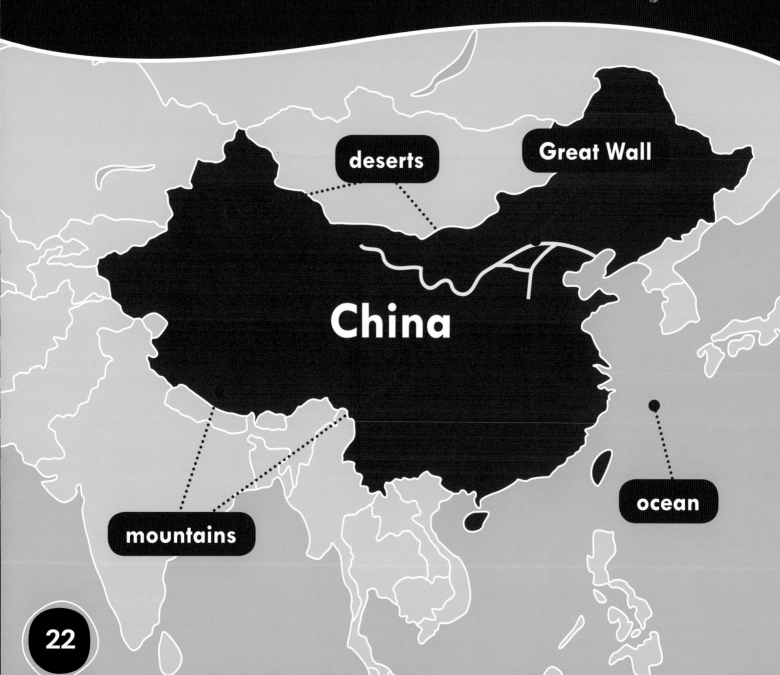

deserts

Great Wall

China

mountains

ocean

22

Picture Glossary

deserts

dry places that get little rain

dumplings

meat or vegetables wrapped in dough

pandas

black and white animals that live in forests and eat bamboo

plains

big, flat pieces of land

Index

Read More

Perkins, Chloe. *Living in . . . China.* New York: Simon Spotlight, 2016.

Sebra, Richard. *It's Chinese New Year!* Minneapolis: Lerner Publications, 2017.

Trueit, Trudi Strain. *Giant Pandas.* Mankato, MN: Amicus High Interest/ Amicus Ink, 2016.

Photo Credits

The images in this book are used with the permission of: © testing/Shutterstock.com, p. 5; © aphotostory/Shutterstock.com, pp. 6–7; © Hung Chung Chih/Shutterstock.com, pp. 9, 23 (bottom left); © SJ Travel Photo and Video/Shutterstock.com, p. 10; © dibrova/Shutterstock.com, pp. 12–13; © aphotostory/Shutterstock.com, p. 14; © hanapon1002/Shutterstock.com, pp. 17, 23 (top right); © baona/iStock.com, p. 18; © Jakrit Jiraratwaro/Shutterstock.com, p. 21; © Red Line Editorial, p. 22; © Jose L Vilchez/Shutterstock.com, p. 23 (top left); © Raywoo/Shutterstock.com, p. 23 (bottom right). Front Cover: © Izmael/Shutterstock.com.